BEYONCÉ

Gareth Stevens
Publishing

By Michou Kennon

RIGHT ON!

Please visit our Web site, www.garethstevens.com. For a free color catalog of all our high-quality books, call toll free 1-800-542-2595 or fax 1-877-542-2596.

Library of Congress Cataloging-in-Publication Data

Kennon, Michou.
 Beyoncé / Michou Kennon.
    p. cm. — (Hip-hop headliners)
 Includes index.
 ISBN 978-1-4339-4788-9 (library binding)
 ISBN 978-1-4339-4789-6 (pbk.)
 ISBN 978-1-4339-4790-2 (6-pack)
 1. Beyoncé, 1981—Juvenile literature. 2. Singers—United States—Biography—Juvenile literature. I. Title.
 ML3930.K66K46 2011
 782.42164092 |a B—dc22

                                    2010023233

First Edition

Published in 2011 by
Gareth Stevens Publishing
111 East 14th Street, Suite 349
New York, NY 10003

Designer: Haley W. Harasymiw
Editor: Therese Shea

Photo credits: Cover, pp. 2–32 (background) Shutterstock.com; cover (Beyoncé) p. 1 Jason Merritt/Getty Images; p. 5 Lunae Parracho/LatinContent/Getty Images; p. 7 SGranitz/WireImage; p. 9 L. Cohen/WireImage; p. 11 Ethan Miller/Getty Images; p. 13 Mike Nelson/AFP/Getty Images; p. 15 Dimitrios Kambouris/WireImage; p. 17 Frank Micelotta/Getty Images; pp. 19, 25 Kevin Winter/Getty Images; p. 21 Pierre-Philippe Marcou/AFP/Getty Images; p. 23 Kevin Mazur/WireImage; p. 27 Evan Agostini/Getty Images; p. 29 Arnold Turner/Getty Images.

Printed in the United States of America

CPSIA compliance information: Batch #CW11GS: For further information contact Gareth Stevens, New York, New York at 1-800-542-2595.

Contents

Just One Name

Some famous people are known by just one name. Beyoncé is one of these people. She is a singer, dancer, and actor.

Beyoncé Giselle Knowles was born on September 4, 1981. She grew up in Houston, Texas.

7

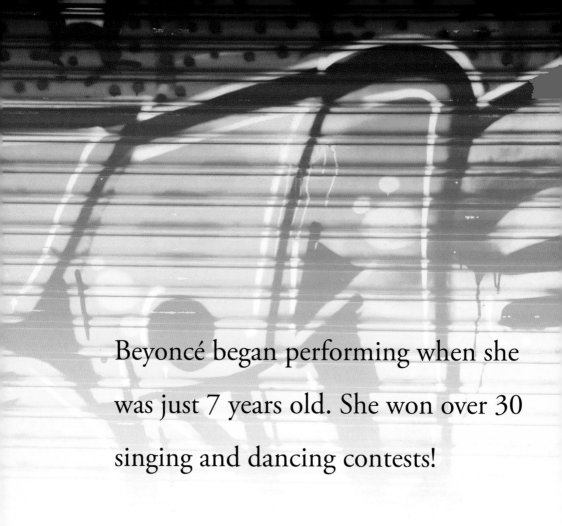

Beyoncé began performing when she was just 7 years old. She won over 30 singing and dancing contests!

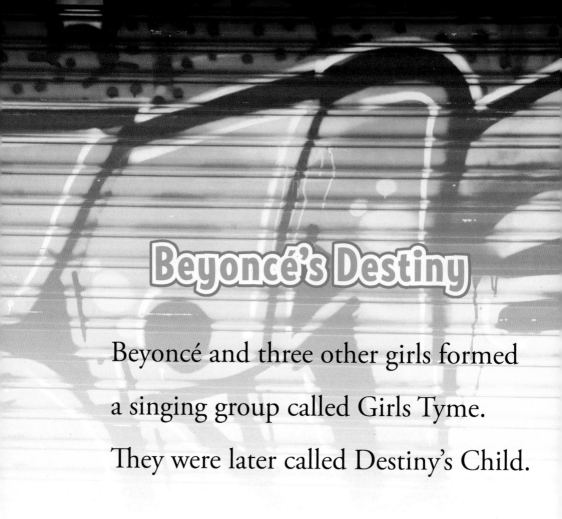

Beyoncé's Destiny

Beyoncé and three other girls formed
a singing group called Girls Tyme.
They were later called Destiny's Child.

arrah Franklin

Kelly Rowland

Beyoncé Knowles

Michelle Williams

11

Destiny's Child became very famous.
Their songs "Say My Name" and
"Bills, Bills, Bills" were big hits.

Kelly Rowland

Michelle Williams

13

Beyoncé and Jay-Z

In 2003, Beyoncé made a solo album.

It was called *Dangerously in Love*.

Beyoncé sang with Jay-Z. Their song was called "Crazy in Love." They later got married!

Jay-Z

17

Beyoncé by Herself

Destiny's Child made one last album in 2004. Beyoncé said they had all grown up. It was time to move on.

Beyoncé's second solo album was called *B'Day*. It came out the day after her birthday in 2006.

21

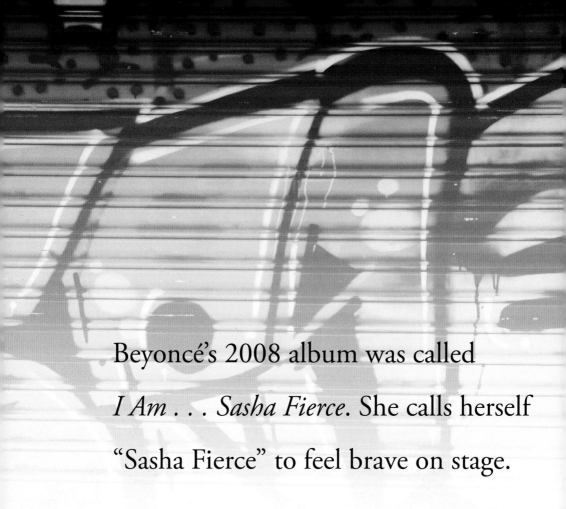

Beyoncé's 2008 album was called *I Am . . . Sasha Fierce*. She calls herself "Sasha Fierce" to feel brave on stage.

In 2010, Beyoncé won six Grammys.
No other woman has won so many
Grammys in one night!

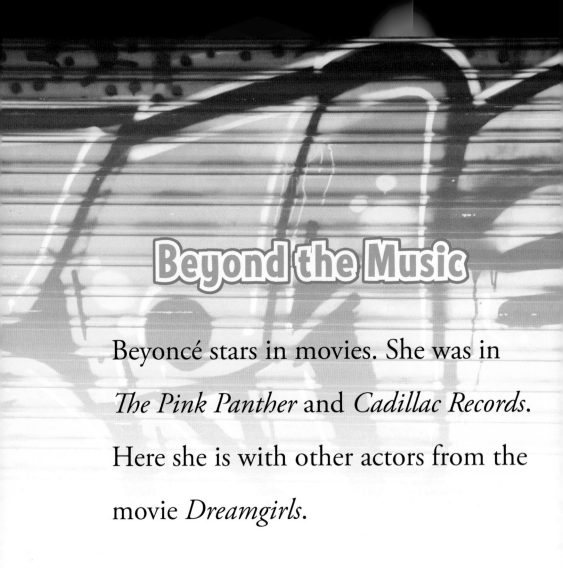

Beyond the Music

Beyoncé stars in movies. She was in *The Pink Panther* and *Cadillac Records*. Here she is with other actors from the movie *Dreamgirls*.

Jennifer Hudson

Anika Noni Rose

27

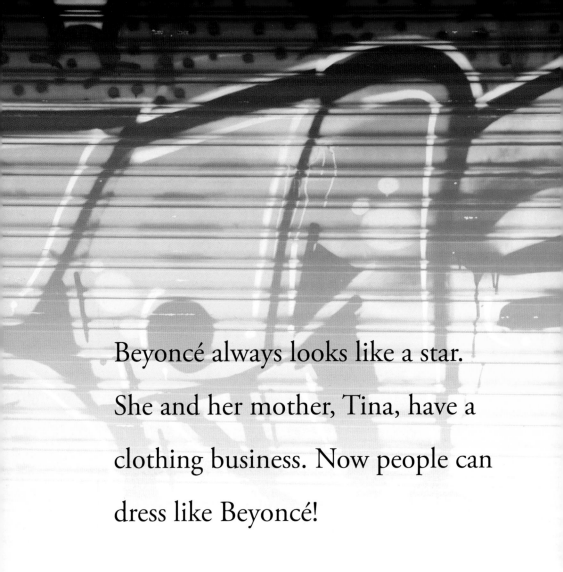

Beyoncé always looks like a star. She and her mother, Tina, have a clothing business. Now people can dress like Beyoncé!

Tina Knowles

29

Timeline

1981   Beyoncé Giselle Knowles is born on September 4 in Houston, Texas.

1998   Destiny's Child comes out with their first album.

2003   Beyoncé's first solo album becomes a hit.

2004   Destiny's Child makes their last album.

2006   Beyoncé's album *B'Day* comes out.

2008   Beyoncé and Jay-Z marry.

2008   Beyoncé's album *I Am . . . Sasha Fierce* comes out.

2010   Beyoncé wins six Grammys.

For More Information

Books:

Dougherty, Terri. *Beyoncé*. Detroit, MI: Lucent Books, 2007.

O'Mara, Molly. *Beyoncé*. New York, NY: PowerKids Press, 2007.

Web Sites:

Beyoncé

allmusic.com/cg/amg.dll?p=amg&sql=11:egj97ip1g7dr

Beyoncé Knowles

www.people.com/people/beyonce_knowles

Destiny's Child

www.destinyschild.com

Glossary

contest: a test of skills among people, usually for a prize

destiny: a force that decides what will happen

fierce: showing strong feelings

Grammy: an honor given to someone for their music

perform: to play or sing a piece of music

solo: alone

Index